KW-409-725

Contents

All the words that appear in
bold are explained in the
glossary on page 30.

WATCH OUT!

In the playroom

Anisa and Alison have been playing with their toys. They begin to tidy up the floor so nobody trips over their toys by **accident**.

Mountfields Lodge C.P. School

At Home

Elizabeth Clark

Photographer: Angus Blackburn

Consultants: The Royal Society for the Prevention of Accidents

Artist: Roger Fereday

Wayland

01208

At Home

Near Water

On My Own

On the Road

Editor: Sarah Doughty
Designer: Loraine Hayes

First published in 1991 by
Wayland (Publishers) Ltd
61 Western Road, Hove
East Sussex BN3 1JD, England

© Copyright 1991 Wayland (Publishers) Ltd

British Library Cataloguing in Publication Data
Clark Elizabeth
At home.
1. Residences. Safety
I. Title II. Blackburn, Angus III. Series
363.1375

HARDBACK ISBN 0-7502-0053-7

PAPERBACK ISBN 0-7502-0598-9

Phototypeset by Dorchester Typesetting Group Ltd
Printed and bound by Casterman S.A., Belgium

Anisa stacks her books neatly on the shelf so that they will not fall and hurt anyone.

Alison ties up her loose shoelaces so she does not trip and fall. Wearing shoes or slippers that fit your feet well will keep your feet safe.

WATCH OUT!

On the stairs

Anisa and Alison walk carefully down the stairs.
They hold on to the **banister** so they cannot fall.

Anisa's mum and dad have put safety gates at each end of the stairs.

This is to stop Anisa's baby brother, Saquib, from falling down them.

Anisa, Alison and Naushee make sure the gates are always safely closed.

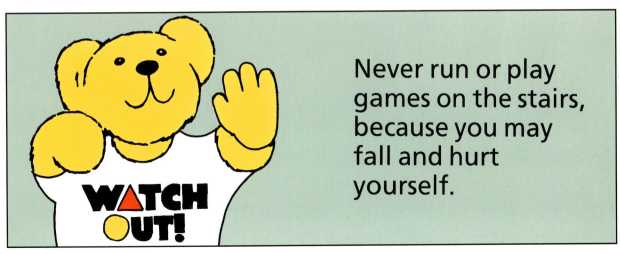

WATCH OUT!

Never run or play games on the stairs, because you may fall and hurt yourself.

In the kitchen

Anisa has been helping her dad to cook tea. She has made cakes.

Dad takes the baked cakes out of the oven for her. Anisa never touches the cooker because it can get very hot and could burn her.

Imran, Anisa's brother, is helping their mum.

Mum cuts the bread into slices with a sharp knife. Imran spreads jam on to each slice.

The children do not touch any of the sharp knives because they could cut themselves.

Everyone is enjoying their tea.

Anisa's mum passes a mug of hot tea to dad very carefully. This is to make sure it does not spill on anybody sitting around the table.

Hot liquids can **scald** which is very painful.

After tea, Anisa helps her mum to wash up. Her mum checks that there are no sharp knives in the soapy water which could cut Anisa.

She also tests the water to make sure that it is not too hot for Anisa.

Anisa has spilt some liquid on the kitchen floor.

She wipes up the liquid at once with a cloth so that nobody will slip and fall.

Anisa and her mum are putting away the dry dishes.

Anisa cannot reach the high cupboard to put the plates away.

She passes them to her mum who reaches up to the cupboard easily.

It is time to clean the kitchen. Dad takes a bottle of cleaning liquid out of a high cupboard.

All the cleaning liquids are kept here, out of reach of the children. Cleaning liquids are **poisonous** and must never be swallowed.

Imran and his friend Gordon are helping mum to put the rubbish in the dustbin.

Imran's mum and dad are careful to wrap up anything with sharp edges so that the children cannot hurt themselves. They do not throw away glass such as bottles which could smash.

Anisa and her mum are putting some dirty clothes in the washing machine.

Anisa and the other children do not go near the machine unless they are helping a grown-up.

Mum is ironing clothes. She is careful where she irons because the iron is very hot and could burn. Someone could also run into the flex and cause an accident.

Naushee sits in a safe place to watch her mum. Naushee does not disturb her when she is busy.

WATCH OUT!

Always keep away from the machines in the kitchen and do not disturb grown-ups when they are using them.

WATCH OUT!

In the lounge

Imran and Gordon want to watch television. Imran's dad puts the **plug** into the **socket** for them and switches on.

The television works by using **electricity**. Electricity must be used carefully to be safe. Always ask a grown-up to help you with electrical equipment.

The family loves to sit in front of the fire in the lounge. There is always a fire-guard in front of it when it is lit.

The children play with their toys on the floor. The toys are never kept on the shelf above the fireplace, as younger children may try and reach them.

WATCH OUT!

Fire!

If a fire starts by accident in your own home, this is what your family must do:

1. Everybody must leave the house immediately. Go straight to a neighbour's house to call for help, or find the nearest telephone box.

2. Dial 999 for the **emergency services**. Ask for the fire brigade. Give the number you are ringing from.

Explain what has happened, giving the address of the fire very clearly. Do not put the phone down until you are told to.

3. Wait for the fire brigade to come and put out the flames. Do not go back into the burning building.

WATCH OUT!

In the garden

Dad unlocks and opens the garden shed. The shed is locked because it contains sharp gardening tools.

Can you see the bottles of liquids which kill weeds and insects? These are poisonous. You must never touch these liquids, or drink from their bottles.

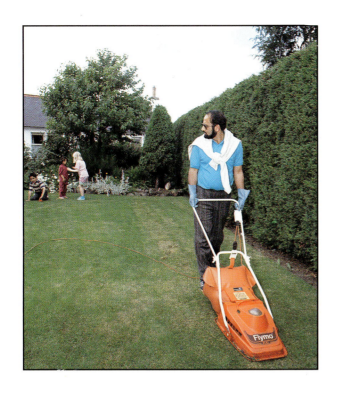

The children keep a safe distance away from dad while he mows the lawn.

The lawn mower is a machine that works by using electricity.

It has a very long flex which could trip somebody up.

When the children play football in the garden, they always keep a safe distance from the windows of the house.

They all wear strong shoes so their feet are safe at all times.

As dad weeds the garden, he warns Anisa about plants which are not safe to taste or to touch with her bare hands.

These plants are poisonous or could hurt you if you touch them:

Highly poisonous	Mistletoe, laurel, rhododendron, autumn crocus, belladonna lily, hydrangea, lily of the valley, nightshade, laburnum, larkspur.
Mildly poisonous	Buttercup, ivy, yew tree, cowslip, sweet pea, daffodil, hyacinth, iris, snowdrop.
Irritates the skin	Foxglove, poison ivy, nettle, lady's slipper, holly tree.

The boys help collect up the weeds and grass.

They are going to make a **bonfire**. Imran's dad will light it with a match while the boys stand back.

WATCH OUT!

Never play with matches because you could start a dangerous fire or cause an **explosion**.

WATCH OUT!

In the bathroom

When Naushee has a bath, her mum always fills the bath ready for Naushee.

Mum checks that the water is not too hot before Naushee climbs in.

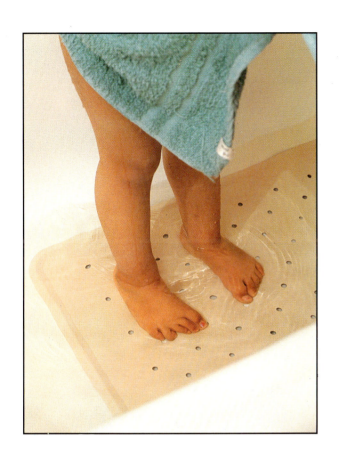

Naushee is about to climb out of the bath.

She stands on the non-slip mat which is in the bath to stop anybody falling over and having an accident.

WATCH OUT!

To cut down on heat and steam, always run the cold tap first, then add hot water until the temperature is warm.

WATCH OUT!

Playing safe

Anisa and Naushee are making posters to tell people how to be safe in the home.

They use blunt-nosed scissors to cut out the paper. The felt-tip pens and crayons they use are all **non-toxic**.

Dad puts the posters up on the wall.

You could draw or paint your own poster to tell people how to be safe at home. Perhaps you could put it on a wall at home or in your classroom at school.

Do you think this house and garden are safe places to be in? How do you think they can be made safer?

Answers on page 32

Glossary

Accident An event which happens by mistake. Sometimes people may be hurt.

Banister The rail running down alongside the staircase. It should always be used to steady anybody using the stairs.

Bonfire An open-air fire where debris can be burned.

Electricity A form of energy (power) for giving heat, light and for working machinery. It is safe if used properly but can be dangerous if not used carefully.

Emergency services The ambulance service, the fire brigade, and the police force are all emergency services. They can be called out in an emergency by dialling 999.

Explosion A loud noise made by something bursting or blowing up.

Non-toxic Not poisonous.

Plug A part joined to a lamp or machine by a flex. It fits into a socket in a wall where electricity flows.

Poisonous This describes something that can harm you if it is taken into the body.

Scald To burn yourself with hot liquid or steam.

Socket A part that a plug fits into, usually in the wall.

Books to read

At Home by Pete Sanders (Franklin Watts, 1989)

Be Careful by Althea (Dinosaur Publications, 1988)

Safety in the Home by Dorothy Baldwin and Claire Lister (Wayland, 1986)

Teach Your Child about Safety at Home by Linda Baillie (Blackie and Son Ltd, 1989)

Teach Your Child about Safety in the Garden by Linda Baillie (Blackie and Son Ltd, 1989)

Notes for parents and teachers

You can do a great deal to prevent accidents in the home by taking some practical safety measures yourself, combined with laying down certain ground rules for your children.

Although safeguarding the home is the adults' responsibility, children can be involved from an early age in tasks which promote safety in the home, such as tidying up their toys from the floor after playing. Under careful supervision, they can gradually begin to take on more responsibility.

To prevent burns, always keep children away from hot surfaces, cookers and oven doors.

Hot drinks and teapots should be kept out of reach. A fire-guard should be used on all types of fire, and children should be warned against touching hot radiators. Keep matches out of the reach of children.

Use safety covers on all unused electrical sockets. Insist that your child must never touch the plugs and sockets in the home and that they should never play with machines that use electricity.

Make sure that household cleaning liquids, medicines and sharp objects are locked away safely. Warn your child about their dangers and insist that they never touch them.

When children are very young use gates at the top and bottom of the stairs. Make sure that they are always safely closed. Encourage your child to walk carefully on the stairs at all times. Fix window locks on to windows, and warn children not to play near open windows.

Never leave a small child alone in the bath or bathroom. Supervise all water play.

If you would like your child to join the Tufty Club to learn more about safety, write to RoSPA at: Safety Education Department Cannon House The Priory Queensway Birmingham, B4 6BS.

Index

Answers to pages 28-29

The house could be made safer in the following ways: a grown-up should always be in the kitchen to watch over boiling pans, the hot iron and its flex. Knives should be kept out of reach of children and empty tin cans thrown away carefully. Handles of the saucepans on the cooker should be turned away from the edges so they are out of a child's reach. Glass should be disposed of properly.

In the lounge, a fire-guard is needed when the fire is lit, and the children's toys should be kept in a safe place, not on the shelf above the fireplace. An overloaded socket is dangerous, and the shelving on the wall should be fixed so that it cannot fall down.

In the bedroom, if bunks are used they should have a ladder and side supports that hold a child safely in the top bed. The heater, the lamp and its flex should be out of the way so that they do not cause any danger to children playing.

In the bathroom, young children should be looked after by a grown-up. Mains electrical equipment should never be used near water. On the stairs the safety gate should be kept shut and any objects that could cause somebody to trip and fall removed from the stairs.

In the garden, gardening equipment and poisonous liquids should be kept well out of the way of children. The children should not be allowed to touch the electrical equipment. Children should play games such as football away from glass which could break. A ladder left against a building is a temptation for a child to climb.